Not For Luck

Not For Luck

POEMS BY **DEREK SHEFFIELD**

WHEELBARROW BOOKS ▪ *East Lansing, Michigan*

Wheelbarrow Books
Michigan State University Press
East Lansing, Michigan 48823-5245

Michigan State University Press
East Lansing, Michigan 48823-5245

Library of Congress Control Number: 2020938148
ISBN 978-1-61186-389-5 (paper)
ISBN 978-1-60917-663-1 (PDF)
ISBN 978-1-62895-422-7 (ePub)
ISBN 978-1-62896-423-3 (Kindle)

Book design by Charlie Sharp, Sharp Des!gns, East Lansing, MI
Cover design by Shaun Allshouse, www.shaunallshouse.com
Cover photo by Marc Dilley

g green press INITIATIVE Michigan State University Press is a member of the Green Press
Initiative and is committed to developing and encouraging
ecologically responsible publishing practices. For more information about the
Green Press Initiative and the use of recycled paper in book publishing, please
visit *www.greenpressinitiative.org.*

Visit Michigan State University Press at *www.msupress.org*

With the publication of Derek Sheffield's collection of poems, *Not For Luck*, the Residential College in the Arts and Humanities (RCAH) Center for Poetry at Michigan State University offers its seventh book in our Wheelbarrow Books Poetry Series. Clearly, we pay homage to William Carlos Williams and his iconic poem, "The Red Wheelbarrow." Readers will remember the poem begins "so much depends upon . . ." that red wheelbarrow. As I write this, across our country and the world, COVID-19 is on the rise. People have been ordered to shelter in place, communities have shuttered their gathering places, restaurants and bars have closed their doors. Pastors are preaching to empty pews. This morning, over 165,000 people in this country have tested positive for the virus. Over 3,000 people have died. We are in unimaginable times. These are the times that call for courage, for community, for cooperation and compassion. They are also times that call for poetry, for writing that inspires, comforts, connects, and speaks to those places in the human psyche that nothing else can reach. Bertolt Brecht asks us,

In the dark times
will there also be singing?
Yes, there will also be singing.
about the dark times.

Derek Sheffield's book, *Not For Luck*, is a book full of singing. He sings of the wonders of the natural world, especially the Pacific Northwest. His poems sing about how the ordinary becomes extraordinary through the act of pure attention, how one moment can cause tectonic shifts; how parents watch their children, and then children become parents themselves; how the love of a father for his daughters changes his world. In his poem, "Middle School," he observes his daughter hop from the car, her focus on her classmates more than on the father she leaves behind. In a sudden turning, she "plucks off her pink headband / with its pink bow dotted with hearts, / checks to see if anyone saw, / and quickly hands it to me." He watches her, in that instant, move from the child he has always known into someone else. "I watch every step I can, holding / the headband with the bow, / a pink U, a horseshoe. Not / for luck, I know, but letting go." For much of our lives we are letting go of things and people we love. If we are not careful with what we have been given, we will be letting go of our world as we know it, the fragile kinship that exists between people and planet. Derek Sheffield sings about those moments. His poems help us understand that luck is of our own making, not some random occurrence. We need to make choices about our actions and our world. We need to make them now. The poet Jorie Graham admonishes us, "For every lie we're told by advertisers and politicians, we need one poem to balance it." In this time of national crisis when lies surround us, *Not For Luck* provides that balance.

As our number of Wheelbarrow Books increases, we hope that our audience increases also. Help us spread the word. In the beginning was the word, and the word became the poem. So much depends upon the collaboration of reader, writer, and poem, the intimate ways we come to know one another. So much depends upon this relationship.

—ANITA SKEEN, *Wheelbarrow Books Series Editor*

n *Not For Luck*, Derek Sheffield achieves something of inestimable value: a trustworthy, convincing voice. A voice, of course, is something we have, but getting it onto the page is another matter entirely. We don't speak in the compressed mode of lyric poetry, even of a colloquial kind, and yet there's something deeply affecting about a poetic voice that sounds effortless, and captures something essential about a speaker. It allows us, over the course of a book of poems, to feel that we've met someone in particular. *Not For Luck* introduces us to a father, a friend, a son, a man deeply embedded in family and community, which is also to say he is a citizen of time, and attentive to passages, growth, and change. He's a deeply engaged observer of and participant in the natural world. One of his most beautiful poems, "The Seconds," is a superbly observed portrait of a wood rat discovered after it's wintered in a shed,

> a big, squirrel-like bulk on my scrap wood,
> the black, unblinking shine of a left eye
>
> tilted toward mine. No glimmer of flight in that orb,
> no twitch of scurry, only the deepest calm
> as if the ages of the earth were taking my measure.
> I felt like a pane of glass . . .

What a masterful passage that is! The diction shifts, as the speaker looks into that steady eye, becoming richly lyrical and more elevated—*glimmer, orb, no twitch of scurry*. And that lets the plainspoken, casual, and unexpected image that follows, *I felt like a pane of glass* . . . arrive with great rightness and force. To be seen by the world, the old, implacable, wordless world, is a bracing, unsettling moment of grace.

—MARK DOTY

for Zoey and Kelsea

and the grains of dust would gather themselves
along the streets and spell out:

these too are your children   this too is your child

—LUCILLE CLIFTON

Contents

Timid as Any Herd Animal

That bright of the blue sky variety
raising every racket of mower
and blower, backhoe and whacker,

not to mention every street's hatch
of after-school slammers and high-pitched
trampoliners. O just a while longer,

a day, maybe three, give them
a rest. Have the hammocks hold fast
and the bark remain in the dog.

Have the thinnest veil of dusk,
fog, or drizzle, call stillness
near, her sister, silence, here.

Stewards at Work

It would be fine to save a few trees,
especially those limber ones that bow
whenever we send our storms.
Some bushes, too. Sedges and grasses
clump agreeably. If we keep those black birds,
our kiss marks on their shoulders
will linger like the coals of that first fire,
remember? Rocks and pebbles, yes,
and boulders with sparkly dots. Night
should continue covering up and day
go on exposing. Let's not forget
those dusky gnats. And that white-faced dog.
Let's have her pace a little longer the length
of every fence, then stop and perk her ears
toward something always coming
that never quite arrives.

2

The Scientists Gather at Mount St. Helens

What does it mean?
asks one as we stand in the wind
of a gray plain and tilt our faces
toward a crater's living steam.

Behind us shrubby trees
grow in patches
among the clean white spikes
of the countless dead.

As they crisscross the air
around our knees, grasshoppers
click their yellow wings.
They mean to find each other

and breed in the heat
we mean to stop making.

April

Now he closes his book.
Slanting light warms
a blue bowl of napkins,
a table specked with crumbs.
He closes his eyes.

Birds. Passing car.
All the leaves lengthening
in their own good time.
Somewhere a bear
opening her eyes.

It is enough today
to walk slowly upstairs
where his daughter curls
in her fuzzy blanket.
It is just right

to bend close and sniff
the lotion of her sleep,
to read in the lines
creasing her neck how
their story might go.

Aubade

He woke and slipped into sleeves in the dark. A few steps
creaked. Clink of spoon as he stirred cream. Made sure
not to trip, the toy prince sprawled by the door.
Left that sleeping house like a thief. "Still,
our girl woke," she says, hours later

while they talk over the phone,
the sun outside beating its gong.
He can hear how it must have
gone, that little voice rising
through the dark room,

"Is it morning time?"
as the window held
the lights of his car

sweeping away
under star scatter.

*The Wren and the Jet at a Research Forest near
Fort Knox, Seventy-One Years since the Bombing of
Hiroshima, Eight Months since the Photo of a Three-
Year-Old Syrian Boy Facedown on a Turkish Beach,
His Red Shirt, His Blue Shorts*

A sound like a plucked banjo as a Carolina wren
lands on a window screen. A parent
and fledgling the last two mornings have made their rounds
of this Kentucky cabin. As the wren pecks
through a beetle pried from a sill, a jet
roars back to the fort. Sound drifts in waves
from the state highway and the beeping of a truck
backing up to the Jim Beam distillery, all that bourbon dribbling
into bottles locals stopped buying when a Japanese concern
bought the company. The scaly feet grip so close
the battering wings make little breaths against the back of my neck.
I'm here to finish the book I can't seem to finish.
"Everybody dies. Get over it." Eighteen years ago
that was Rick, who lives in language. But those waves
kept washing in all night, kept finding that boy
the way a parent returns to a fevered child.
The sand keeps spilling from his open mouth.

Fish Like These

People crowding the darkened room
use their air for words
like *Look!* as they press their hands
to a topaz light. Glass divides
the aquarium, but through
the perfectly flat chill—
Here!—they can almost feel
the gilled and tentacular, breathe
their symphony of blending rays
and bending weeds. *More than meets the eye,*
says a woman, smiling in her secret
and standing apart in a blue vest
to tell the half-truth before them.
See that rockfish with scarred sides
and a notched fin? Heads all turning
toward a spiny length of scales
moving in coppery swishes.
Disease took his eye, and the other fish
wouldn't stop lunging for the empty socket.
At the tank's end, he flutters into a turn.
Anymore, fish like these don't grow on trees,
so we pulled him out, put him under,
and stitched a glass eye to his ocular bone.
With dull glimmers he approaches,
and they—I mean *we*—shuffle and squint,
snap our gum and purse our lips,
and cannot tell which eye
peers into its own blind skull
and which sees our outstretched hands.

hitch

this ceaseless going you
follow when you
follow a stream
back into the hills
purls and moils
wrinkles into flats its
glassy aim
breaking to re-
shape every slope it is
bound to flow
and crumple each
try to make sense
of whirl and glint
and hold it
what's this
gliding your way
on that lit skin
but a white dab
of a day moth stuck up-
side down, wings full spread
and legs like sutures
crookedly struggling
and you who have
seen this many times
this time are grabbing
for a stick
to reach with
and miss and miss
again and stumble-
jog to try once no
twice more before you

8

lift it dripping
into the air
even as you catch
a glimpse of yourself
in the streaming sheen
holding a bite-
sized hitch in earth's weft
for you do not stop
your dimpled twin
from swiping it
onto your finger
and peering into
the pinpricked black
of its globed eyes
which must see you
multitudinously
the you who has killed
and eaten and licked
his greasy fingers the you
who has hurt others
and borne grudges
and the you who will again
and this one
who walks upstream
to the tallest pine tree in sight
to divert a little life
for once at least this one
onto the bark where it crawls
wing-shivered into one
of the many furrows
puzzling its way up
past how many flakes

and branches breaking
how many rays of light
and how many needles
flaring all the way up
                    to where a wisp of cloud
                    in the whole blue sky
                    floats

Traveling Again through the Dark

—for Bill and all

Having flown from their far cities
and checked in downtown, the ecopoets
gather at the university to elucidate
the nature of this new nature poetry.

One taps her mic, "Can you hear me?"
and they are off with a talk that leads them
from the faces of Personification Peak,
down a road that curls along the curves

of Mimesis Creek and corkscrews them
ever deeper: "I really hate that poem
where the speaker runs over a deer
and gets out to find she's pregnant—

you know that one?" Many heads nodding.
"It's when he says, 'I thought for everybody.'"
"What hubris!" says another. "Why's he thinking
for *me*?" And after a third agrees—frowning

through his goatee—they work as one
to shove the poem out of their consideration.

Good Girl

In 1957, Laika, a mongrel dog from the streets
of Moscow, became the first living animal in orbit
when the Soviets launched Sputnik 2.

Horoshaya devochka, they said,
leading her down bright halls
to bowls of food and water.
Little Bug, they said, patting her head.
Little Lemon gazing up at them,
turning her belly to the smooth, clean hands
taking her measurements.
Little Curly's numbers, of course,
counting down from the second they found her
to the seconds her respirations and heart
went blazing up a blue sky.
From her body

harnessed at the center
of that long forceful roar,
from each place they'd shaved her,
colored wires shivered with data,
but nothing could show
how they became we and she ours,
the fur and love and living breath
we sent away.
Into that mute black,

whistles and kiss sounds
turning, each whiff of a white coat's
swish, all our kind

and beautiful faces drifting closer
in the floating moments

her eyes went blank.

Daughter and Father in Winter

"Clap like this!" she says,
and we clap the stuttering

snaps of the kindling
coming to life in the stove

we have scooted close to,
to play the game she makes

as the fire goes.
"Raise your arms!"

and we move like flames
waving *hello*

and *goodbye* to the snow
outside our windows.

"Now close your eyes!"
and she gets us to bunch

ourselves into balls and hold tight
inside the heat's growing belly.

"Don't peek!" And I don't
stop peering into the dark.

Silence. Ash.
"Look!

It's snowing in my eyes!"
"Yes," I say, opening mine,

"and I'm starting to freeze!"
She opens her eyes and sees

the frost in my beard. Her laughter
ignites another fire.

Think of the language we two, same and not-same,
might have constructed from sign,
scratch, grimace, grunt, vowel:

Laughter our first noun, and our long verb, howl.

—MAXINE KUMIN

The Math of Two

One plus one is more
        than two rooms
painted periwinkle and celery,
        more than potty talk
and shouting things you'd like to
        unshout—one day
your marriage the slick reek
        leaking out the sides
of a split diaper, the next
        two powdered and bath-
warm cheeks. One plus one
        adds up in the play, just now,
on the face of the younger one,
        her slight eyebrows raised
and mouth an oval zero as she clutches
        the bedside to watch her sister
count apples in a book.
        Numbers, words, everything
is y, especially her sister
        who kicks her hand,
yelling, "No!" so that
        she plops down and cries
and shakes her hands as if waving
        goodbye by the power of two.
It will be x number of years
        divided by x number of lines drawn
before each understands she is
        a fraction of the beauty and oddity
in the other. They may not even
        figure this until all that remains
of us is what they equal.

Now her sister laughs and points,
and though she doesn't know why,
she laughs, too.

Bedtime Story

> He set the sun and the moon
> to be earth's lamplight, lanterns for men.
>   —Beowulf

Hinged to the glowing pin
        of a porch light, a blurring
twister of moth wings beyond the window

draws the silhouettes of two
        bath-scented sisters.
At a word from their father, they patter

up the stairs, nude as moon babies,
        and come floating
down in brightly colored nightgowns.

Another word and they flit away
        and back to breathe
whiffs of toothpaste and plead

for him to let them be
        a little longer.
He could let dawn find him

just as he is, weary and sprawled
        and watching as they stand
on their toes to follow the same pallid

and whirling blaze that caught him
        long ago, a lamp
by a mountain lake, his father and the laps

of dark water. Yes, the skittery wings
        of their fingers at the glass,
little taps, a while longer, please.

The Science of Spirit Lake

It's the water's pulse through line
and rod that judders in his hands, in fish
after fish whip-thrashed into air, into arms
and body and day's heat, all day, day
after day, all summer, and into the net

where she stands to her waist
in the lake's cool sway, and the lake
in lit wrinklings letting go as she
wades their catch to shore and quickly
kneels and lays it flat to her measured board,

pinned beneath her sun-lined hands
as she bends to sex, clip, and scrape
while keeping it alive (gills fluttering
like the dream-caught eyes of children)
before she turns and splashes back.

And each, as she stops to let her arms
fall open, hangs there as if unable to let go
of her grasp or remember its own truth
of unnumbered shadows. When the life
(from who knows where) comes finally

shudderingly back and it shiver-flits away,
a few scales are left to slowly tumble
and flash and become, like the clear seconds
it takes to watch them, indistinguishable
from the restless body that holds them.

For Those Who Would See

the swift and ceaseless sprinkler whirling
and flinging its bright globes

drop by drop has filled a blue bowl
left out on the lawn. The little pool
formed by that embrace never stops

breaking and regathering—winks of calm
coming between bouts of splattering—

and in the way the pool accepts
each troubling drop so it becomes
the surface that in the next instant

shatters at the next and so on,
this is also clearly a matter of light

splashed and light
scattered in all directions
for anyone who happens to be watching.

Emissaries

ROCK CREEK

Early sun and birdsong found us
checking our map in the gravel pullout
Chris had marked at Hugo's Milltown hole.
What you know about knots?
Andy took my line to teach me
the blood and clinch, muttering
as he licked and bit,
You get that first hit, you'll know.

I waded into a froth-specked swirl
in a pair of glue-patched waders
Dwight had loaned me back in Wenatchee
and tried to remember to call the pole a rod
and wave it the way Steve did in my yard, to haul
like Whitney, to tuck and mend to make the fly
a truer kind of lie, and, though I had the best riffles,
my thumb and hat were my only bites.

CLARK FORK

We took Chris's advice the next day
and stripped streamers in measured half-
loops across the current. While Andy
brought five to hand, my hands
twitched like water striders through snags
and thistles, tangles like thoughts
twisted into grudges. And still I lost two
Buggers and an olive Zonker.

FLINT CREEK

It was when our last water on our last day
held my neoprened thighs in its cool,
complete grasp, and my ears
were awash with thirty hours
of wavering rushes and laps, a tug
in my legs that wouldn't let go,

a thousand kinds of round
in the stones under my feet, the squish
and suck of silt, a hundred elk
turning their shaggy, sorrel heads
at our breeze-borne voices,

smells of sun-lathered stone
and sand, cottonwood shade mixed
with leaf murmur, some dead thing's
bottom-snagged skin billowing
like a white guidon,

feeling again in my hands the slick,
torsional body of a pinked westslope cutt,
and pearly light playing across every ripple
widening through sleep as I drifted off
after lunch to water chatter and woke

to the first inklings of a storm and saw
in drops spotting the pale bed of stones
the aggregate beauty of every trout
and star-clotted night.

It was when a yellow warbler tumbled leaf-like
from a streamside willow to nearly snap
my dropper before landing with a tap
on my rod tip, jittery droplet
of an eye flicking toward mine and away

and back, its feathers
emissaries of the first rays
ever to touch these waters to life.
When it leapt at the word
that slipped from my mouth
and flew quick as a fish
from an opening hand—
I knew.

Emergency

A doe sets her left
front hoof onto
the road as I roll
to a stop—and
watch her through
the windshield take
a second sleek
step as another
doe appears. More
slow steps, and
pause as they turn
dark, unblinking
eyes toward two
cars pulling up
behind me.
A few seconds
is all it takes—
the deer going on,
nearly there,
my foot lifting
from the brake—when
two others appear
and the glint
of another car.
And I press
my foot more
firmly to the brake—let
them be one
thing ahead of
ours—and let us
get where we need to

watching the silky
pistons of their steps,
my hazard lights
pulsing like a
cornered heart.

First Grade

Sunday afternoon and she looks up
from her drawing, wants to know
if I know the game where you put
your head down and thumb up

until someone picks you.
"Yes," I say, across the room and half-
listening. "Well, I always pick my friends
but they never pick me." I pause

in the middle of a sentence.
"Who are your friends?"
"Everyone!" she says, as if I had asked
one plus one or the color of the sky.

Sunlight draws a skewed rectangle
across the floor. "I see," I say
and let my notebook close, seeing
children in rows, heads on desks,

her big ears poking through sandy hair,
listening for a step or a breath. "Yes,
I remember that game." And I stand
and walk over to find the outline of her hand

plunging through a white sky.

Her Calling

"Have to call someone,"
she says, and dials a bright song
on the fat buttons of her plastic mermaid phone
as we cross the parking lot of the school
that has just taken her pinching, kicking,
hugging, sorry-saying sister
for the next nine months, the one
she loves best in the world
and hasn't been without
since she was out of her mother.

It's not her sister, though,
she talks to as I buckle her, but Echo,
that black Lab our neighbors
were always calling back across the road
until a screech one night made silence
repeat itself across the valley. "Echo!"
she says. "We've been looking for you!"
And she goes on catching up with that shadow
of a dog until we pass a tree full of crows
and wants to know if I know
what they're saying.

Last week her phone started ringing
all by itself, right after she sat on it.
"Oh, no! It's Mia!" she said.
I've never seen Mia, of course, or any of the others,
but knowing her through reports
that begin, "You won't believe what Mia said!"
I said don't answer, but it's a good thing she did—
turned out to be Curly wearing a Mia mask
and calling from Luna's house.

This happened
not long after she saw her baby self
on the computer and she called that bald dribbler
to say she didn't talk good. Now she's tapping
the back of my seat. We're almost home,
and it's my turn, so I steer
with one hand and dial with the other
an operetta of *bonk, ding,* and *boing*
into the future, to a time that may come for her
as it did for me, when her days turn up
empty as the eyes of a doll
left behind, her heart a tangle
of crow cries.

"Here," I say,
and hand her the phone, for who
better to recall that possible future self
to the inexhaustible dream that is her calling?
May she keep herself
the way a shell cupped to an ear, no matter
how far or broken, never lets go
of ocean. "For you."

Monsters

It waited for the happy ending
        to end, for the kiss
and light touch, waited for the door
        to click, her breathing
even, and then, before the stuck-
        open, night-lit eyes
of her stuffed animals, and despite
        her pink blanket
in her arms, it took her.
        We'd made a show of checking
the closet and under the bed,

        but not until months later,
in a far city where a team of neurologists
        sent her to the third floor
of a children's hospital, did we see.
        As she lay with wires
tied into a multicolored cord dangling
        umbilically from her gauze-
wrapped skull to the wall,
        as night fell
through eight days of nights, we saw
        something like a breeze
enter her sleep, then her eyes
        fly open at a gust
heaving through her chest, her eyes
        two blips of black water
unseeing us. Then legs
        jerked and arms shivered up
like plant stalks in fast-forward,
        desperate petals of fingers un-
clenching. Then one—two—

three convulsive gasps
and the gurgle of a squeezed fish.

This brute puppetry
of our girl's body every night,
these seizures of bone
and blood stuttering—over how many
months?—and growing
more shake and snap, more gouged
in epileptic gray,
while one floor below, we were sliding
a finger down a page
or thigh, or letting our eyes
close, possessed by our certainty,
even laughing at times
when we promised
no such thing.

We Could See

          If we mapped this
mountain creek's channel
          over many seasons of spill
and flood   gravel

          and jam   we could play
those maps back
                    like the flip pictures we drew
in rooms of another age
          to let one more hour
                    slip by

and we could see
          without a doubt
                              that jabbed snake
writhe before our eyes
          and would hear   of course
                    not a sound
          in such a scream

while in our cities
                    bright glasses of iced water
          like nothing
kept appearing across tabletops

The Skookum Indian

Since 1921, Wenatchee, Washington

Above the Dollar Tree those dark eyes
shift side to side all day and all night.
Now and then one of them winks.

He's a giant motorized head, this Indian of ours,
with a cartoon nose and long black braids.
Above the Dollar Tree those dark eyes

shadow changing lights wherever we drive,
googly holes pinned to a wobbly sky
where now and then one of them winks.

A grin big as a sunset that won't die
promises a brand of apples long dead
beside the Dollar Tree. (Those dark eyes.)

We mostly forget, but out-of-towners
love to pose beneath those red cheeks.
Now and then one of them winks

back. His name means *strong* or *monstrous*.
The tilt of his single feather never alters.
Above the Dollar Tree those dark eyes:
now and then one of them winks.

In Nez Perce Country with Kevin

On a narrow path
along the Snake,
my friend and I
walk between
the canyon wall
and the river's
streaming, sharing
what we know
of the tribe whose
steps have fallen
before ours.
We keep passing
tapering, basaltic
slides, all
breaks and edges.
They look like
they might sweep
through us
at a word
or click.
We walk on
until Kevin
stops and bends
down. In his palm
held out,
an arrowhead.
With one finger,
he rubs the dust
from the black
of shattered water
still sharp and down
the centuries
shining.

A True Account of Wood-Getting
from up the Chumstick

with apologies to Doug Heckman

Crossing a steep slope of brushy second-growth
I put my hand out for leverage and felt it
give, and gave a shout, and Heckman
turned to take the snag's notched top
with his forehead. When he looked up
blood gleamed between the fingers
of his leather glove, and more dripped
a trail back to the truck. As the doctor needled
the first stitch, he asked what happened.
"By the time you figure *all* the costs," he said
to me in my work clothes and saw stink,
"you're better off buying your wood."
Said Heckman, holding his head perfectly still
and eyeing that needle, "Well, that's dumb.
Then you'd lose all the fun." Not a prick
of irony, but the bright slice of a meteor
across the exact night I was gazing into.
Another seven stitches, a short drive,
and he took the stacking so I could halve
the skinny rounds of the snag that blazed him.
That's what I see when I see him now—a way
ahead as clear as his. The rest of that day
the bandage stuck through heave and sweat
and we kept at it for two cords of heft and swing
and grapple and heap, moving our bodies
as well as we could through all we hauled
out of those woods, and getting the work done
as the land split the light of a beautiful wound.

C-3PO

The coop's door swings open
and where we reach our hands
not eggs but a sun-colored, unmoving bulk
of chicken. She's asleep or mid-lay
the way she looks with her shut eye
and tucked neck, but is to our pokes
stiff as molded plastic.

A year ago we'd learned the right heat
to keep the five balls of fluff and *cheep*,
and as they grew beyond our palms,
what they could and couldn't eat.
Now one daughter cries, turns away,
and the other keeps petting dead feathers.

They can be drained by a single bite,
said a neighbor, but no sign of weasels,
and I say nothing of such teeth. Just as
last winter when I swept fresh snow over spatters
of blood then helped my girls hang flyers
until we agreed our cat had found a new home.

We bury the chicken beside the garden,
each offering a sprinkle of pine shavings
before the shovels of dirt eclipse
her bright feathers. We close our eyes
and bow our heads and say we loved her,
and as we look up, we see the others
sprinting toward us in their funny,
wobbling way. They want to say goodbye,
we say, Darth, Leah, Chewy, and Rey
tilting their heads toward us and back

to the ground, making their tentative *crows*
and lingering *coos*. As one they begin stepping forward
to scratch back the loose soil over their fellow,
aiming repeated pecks by swivels
of their meticulous, oil-drop eyes.

Let this be goodbye
to the chicken. But let these daughters stay
in their belief she loved us, too, a little longer,
and not notice the machinery
of those clock-hand necks.

40

were there trees in those places
where my father and my mother were born
and in that time did
my father and my mother see them

—W. S. MERWIN

What Happens

Once dandelions were tests of loving.
When he picked one, he twirled it
to a friend's chin and she to his.
Always gold dabbed them both
butter lovers. Any pale fluffs
of seed that floated by
they caged in fingers
and sent breath and wants into
before opening their hands
to watch them dwindle
down the wind, the years.

Up through every lawn,
they rise again, hers,
where she bends to pick
each white globe by its stem
and carry it as carefully
as wedding crystal to the trash,

while he strides across his
in time with his neighbors,
cranking out white, semicircle sprays
of chemical-smelling granules.

Back and forth they go, breathing
the ghosts of their wishes.

It Wasn't the Laundry

The father could not have known
the woman he'd hired to be with his children
while he followed his work to far cities
would bring such pain. It wasn't the laundry,
floors, or sack lunches, not the dropping off
or picking up that did it. It came after dinner
when she called them to a game, and kept calling
until even the boy closed the latest in a series
of books where he'd been since his mother
had left, and unlocked his door
and walked downstairs to get it over with.

With that woman and his two sisters, he sat around
the little-used dining room table to connect four
colored disks or link cool tiles with clicks across
the polished wood or lay down a card:
"UNO!" The pain they learned began in queries
about their day and help with fractions, in how
to stitch a rip and fry potatoes. It grew in flowers
from her garden, the blue wheels of bachelor's buttons
and purple-hearted Sweet William. (Do we live
in your days, Mother? Where this time, Father?) Their faces
over years around that table starting to smile,
to fly into laughter. Now that woman, neither

mother nor father, lies in a distant bed. Different people
on different shifts lift spoons to her mouth,
change her sheets. There is no more calling or hearing
and no games but the one in her eyes turned toward
a window, where twice a day twilight touches her face.
Being neither day nor night, but a little of both,

and both end and beginning, here is the hurt
their father did not know he was buying
in every check he left on the kitchen counter.

Exactly What Needs Saying

There's Father at the kitchen counter,
and there he is at the stovetop
where a steel pot's beginning to bubble.
Now he's picking up and putting away,
now rinsing plates, for tomorrow
it begins again. It never stops.
Your whole life with him, and now
when you visit, his standing at the sink, face
clouded in steam, hands carefully drying
each glass as you sit in the family room
sharing your life with your sisters.
It keeps going, this hiding behind
the sweeping and wiping, this acting
as if the crumbs you might scatter
or the dirt on your shoes is what matters,
this pretending not to see you
rolling around on the floor with your toddler daughters,
one after the other over the years
plopped on that same red rug, shaking her hands
and crying as you crooned, "Use your words."
It never stops, this reserve of doing what needs doing,
and his father before, always going or gone
to harrow or hammer. And what about you,
alone in the dark of morning as you like,
here in your house on a side street
while your family sleeps on. How much longer
will it be before you stop doing
and start saying exactly what needs saying?

Abortion Wish

Wherever you are, whomever,
I would you were never
begun, Half-Brother. Not for anything
you did, but for how she
was done when you began.

Autumn's leaves clawing
the gravel drive he walked out on, that boy-
father after she told him
about it, about you. Nothing for her to do
but let her father pay the fare

to a charity in Portland
where she lived with other fucked girls
from other single-schooled towns.
There they studied for the life
a GED would bring,

learning to lower their eyes
as the lives inside them grew.
The night you were triggered I would void
so she never had to be that
alone: legs pressed wide

in a room full of gloves and masks
as she heaved you out
in sheet-twisting pain. With you
undone, no baby to not be touched
when a nurse held you to the glass

(she thought it a kindness)
while our mother—still in bed, still

bleeding at the rip, dried fig
of a smile on her beautiful girl face—
took in your ruddy cheeks, dark hair,

your shut eyes, the little features
she would come back to all her life,
what she went looking for
when nothing seemed to be looking for her.
Maybe a doctor or actor. How rich

or handsome by now? She never knew,
for you, like all the faces
when she went home, turned away.
Didn't you know, Brother? You were the one
who carried her happiness.

John Carter of Mars versus the Void

No, I said to my two friends
who begged me to come out, the front door
open to the rare wonder of snow
where we lived then. I'd been reading all morning
the latest book in a sci-fi series

I couldn't imagine living without.
They tried and tried to change my mind.
Just as I found my place in that other land,
snowballs slammed into the door. Slushy,
hard-thrown missiles, they pounded

until I thought the wood would crack.
The way they sounded they could have been rocks,
and still they did not stop. This
is my response to one of those boys,

friend I've known longest on this planet
who wakes me thirty-eight winters later
with a letter about a family and career and a great lack
that has plunged into his—, and I see the knife
of his cursive *f* in "life." He says he barely has the will
to change a light bulb. I tell him that I know
it's not a reddish speck

glimmering in the night sky that would take him,
not a beautiful princess abducted
by green, many-armed, tusk-faced Martians
wielding bejeweled swords, but simply
and utterly, the nothing all around it.
I wept long after the last blow.
When I opened the door, no one,

no marks above bits of scattered melt.
I tell him I know now it wasn't him. It was
the need to accept the gift of the bodied world
knocking that day. Each impact's freezing starburst

was not cruelty, I say, but the hammered truth
that I would have to live
my earthbound life and love and suffer
my own series of crystalline moments and what
was I going to do about that?

Notes, Descending

She wants nothing to do with spiders
           but that's what her hands turn into
in each tentative finger that lifts
           and lowers across the keys.
Like daddy longlegs, he thinks, as he sits
           near the piano, right
where she likes him to stay and be
           the stillness and silence
she sends her notes through.

           Up the scales they go,
and the strings, as he lets his eyes close, grow
           shorter and brighter
until he hears the clinks metal spoons
           make, and sees again
the baby in the high-chair, her gossamer hair
           and *O* of mouth from which
shining lines of spittle wobble,
           tiny maestro hands bringing two
silvery wands together . . . *clink clink* . . .

           She always insisted he
be the one to push her on the swing,
           and when he'd stop
and pick her up, she'd cry and shake her arms
           and kick her legs, her wish
to always be dangled by those thin strands
           of swoop and swish . . .

. . . how long have the notes
           been descending,

he wonders, opening his eyes
        to see how angular
she sits, her thin, straight shoulders,
        head tilted just so.
No more tears or fits. He knows his part,
        a father's art of staying
caught near the center of her
        diaphanous arrangement
quivering about them.

A Song for Today

for Stellarondo and Rick Bass

We've gathered in the hall
    of an ex-cathedral
for fiction in concert with song,
    a little banjo mixed
with people and their predicaments,
    and we find ourselves
surrounded by a brutal gift,
    His sculpted flesh
in stages in the walls, His story
    and ours part
of the old tune that begins in silence
    as the red-haired cellist
takes up a saw, a silvery ribbon
    of toothed light
she presses to her thigh
    and leans into. Down

    goes her bow and up
climbs the shrill wavering of a siren,
    urgencies strung
with wooing, the pledge of flesh
    coming from every
wet wreck. Her bow rises and back
    we go to a fire's heat
and cave walls restless with animals
    we sketched long ago
into being. They have never stopped
    watching from their eyes

in the dark our changing, our mouths
        over time growing
thin enough to make blades of our words.
        Not here, not them,
we say. We are more. We rise,
        they stay.

Idaho, Maybe

> Northern Idaho was the notorious base of operations
> for the Aryan Nations, who'd turned to Hayden Lake
> because of its isolation and general absence of non-
> whites. Once a year, white supremacists from around
> the world would converge there for a big conference.
>
> —Mother Jones

"I don't know. Idaho, maybe?"

was an odd thing to overhear
from the hallway for we were in
Idaho, opining on assonance
in poetry month. What question,
we wondered, for such an answer,
maybe,

"Where do white supremacists go to die?"

What a strange notion, we thought, supreme,
as if such a thing could be so black
and white.

We did feel sorry for our state, though.
Imagine trying to get everyone to think
of great heaps of russet potatoes

instead of hate, so many tank-topped whites
blasting death metal in the woods,
rubbing at the hours with their rifles.

I remember sitting on the edge

of my bunk bed, watching the words

Diana Ross
and the Supremes

turn in the middle of grooves
shining like black water as they sang,

"What the world needs now is love, sweet love."

I could hardly imagine something so humble
and powerful. I listened and waited
to be something more than eight,
to learn the white foot I kept for luck
had been cut from a real rabbit.

Elvis's "All Shook Up"
was my other 45, his swagger
filling my basement room
like dark walnut. It would be twenty years
before I heard him described
as a white man who sang black.

"Where's the King now?"

is another possibility.
If he were here, maybe he could sing
a blackish dream for Idaho, Idaho, maybe,
and the many fruits of our awfully glorious home.

Contextual Education

Wenatchee, Washington

"He wouldn't make us like *monkeys!*"
says a student in the front row.
"Cause he made us in *His* image."
She laughs and turns to check
for smiles and nods. The professor
stands by the whiteboard
where he has written the word
adaptation. He's thinking of all
the lessons, like similes,
that have appeared in black ink
across this space,
and that have, like species,
gone. He cannot help
but see her in the church van
on the field trip, pretending
she doesn't know she's the pretty one
who doesn't know exactly
what's happening inside the boy
beside her when she tosses
her pink-streaked hair and blows
a word across his ear. In the room's silence,
she shows them what she means
by turning her hands into big ears
and wagging her head.
They wonder what sort
of experiment they are as their professor
turns off the lights and clicks
a chimp's face onto the screen.

No one says a thing
at the god looking back
from those brown, sad eyes.

Still Time

In a wide
and motionless circle, nine

Chinook salmon
below a stilled spillway,

nose to tail-fin, wait,
faint flutterings rounding their backs

in place, each moment
slipping (a white bubble

up from the dark) through the clock face
they make of creek water,

a count we might mistake
as ours.

What Will Keep Us

for Katie and Kelsea on the Save Our Coast Hike

The coast is never saved. It's always being saved.

—Peter Douglas

Every pack-heavied step over sand hoppers
        and weed-slicked rocks, through driftwood scatters
and the chill of tidewaters, over wooded headlands
        as wildfires blaze north, south, east—every step says
stay. "I know mermaids aren't real," Kelsea says, "but Daddy,
        look," holding a whip of bull kelp whose lightbulb face
is a brown-green eye under ribbons of translucent hair.
        We trudge our miles, stepping over oscillating
anemones in sunlit pools to pause at Hole-in-the-Wall
        and let their tentacles tongue our dipped fingers.
And what's this holographic sheen? Not the oil
        we would keep from this shore, and not plastic,
we see, just a rainbow's iridescence beaming
        from a plant. Over teeth of barnacled rocks poking
from pools of sand crabs and sculpin, through foamy
        maroons, emeralds, violets—tangles of surfgrass
and lettuce cushioning our steps—we hike, flies parting
        briefly for our ankles as we take in the gleaming curve
of the otter's tail as she rises and dives into clear
        shallows, a pliable needle threading us and them, water,
land, and rippled sky where the numberless legs
        of sandpipers twiddle their skittery flocks always
just ahead. For even the reek-slap of rot from a carcass
        too far gone for ravens or gulls we hike, for our own
place among the eaters and the eaten pricking at us
        as we see how wide the jawbone, how long and curved

the fangs. For the piping stutter of a crow-mobbed eagle
        landing on a shaggy bough, for the lightest touches
of day mist on our skin and our headlamps
        in the night lighting the tracks of slugs silvering up
every spruce trunk's loom. We hike for what will keep us
        if we keep it. On a bare stretch of sand ahead, a boulder
splits into two bear cubs whose dark heads swivel our way
        before they turn as one toward the woods and lope
out of sight, to go on in the multitudinous dream we need
        to be beyond our reach. Out past the breaking lines
of waves we can just glimpse through binoculars,
        where the rounded humps of humpbacks slope one way
and gray whales the other, sixty-some otters floating
        on their backs have knit themselves into a living net—
weft, warp, leg, paw—kelp blades fixed by holdfasts
        to the deepest rocks. What is it they catch
in their drift of sleep amid mists and rolling webs
        of stars? Far enough where, if we fail, the drills
will rise. And what now as they ride day's swells in
        and out of sight in the rhythm of our own breathing?
Our hike ends at the beginning of what the map calls
        Wedding Rocks, where people of the Makah long ago
carved the round faces of sun and moon among fishers
        and fish, a whale, an orca. What feelings
spilled through them as they knelt in these same
        unceasing sounds of waves, chip after chip falling away?
We trace the grooves with our fingers, five centuries
        of wind laced with the wet snorts and hunger cries
of passing animals. Kelsea kneels over some new swirl
        of shell and exclaims. Katie says not a word, drawing
with her stick something in the sand we can't yet see.

There was a sunlit absence.

—SEAMUS HEANEY

The Empty Road Full of People

Everything looks right in this photo
of the 1910 Fourth of July parade
taken from a rooftop near Palouse.
Black-and-white world of hand-lettered windows,
men in hats on crowded walks, and power poles
striding toward a bright horizon. Everything
except the foreground where townsfolk
are not facing the oncoming displays
of first-ever automobiles, only
the empty road before them.

See those splotches
across the packed dirt? That's where
the Okanogans and Wenatchis went.
First they were there, in vests and feathers,
liquid moments riding horses,
then the slow swipe of a thumb.

He wanted them gone, that photographer,
white as I am, ghost bent over
negatives in the dark. In celebration
of his independence the tribes had come.
What made him want to undo that?
What was it he saw or didn't see
to smear their faces into stains?

A hundred years later his failure appears
in my old student come back
from the arts school, her long black hair
not vanishing but sliding across her shoulders
as she leans from her chair with the mini sally bag
she has made. *Celly bag*, she says,

and points to the woven image
of the cell phone, her near-smile the same
I've seen in her uncle and others of her tribe.

Here they are, brought forward by her hands.
Here she is, as if years hadn't gone by,
asking me to stand beside her
as she raises her phone aimed back.

for Carly Feddersen

The Nature of Time Was What
They Were Talking About

for the topic of their next essay
when a red-haired girl pointed
to the clock on the wall ticking,
they noticed, four minutes fast.
The future is here! she said

and flashed a smile.
From another row,
a boy's proclamation—
Numbers are how we know it!—
sent someone into a countdown.

But really, they all said, and held up
their twenty-four hands
so their teacher could see
their twenty-four phones.
The bell rang four minutes fast

in their sleep that night.
The moon had not been mentioned,
nor anything about leaves
or cold. Still

a chalky, bare-limbed light
seeped through every window
to their pillows

where their eyelids twitched
with something like a dream

flapping rapidly away.

At the Log Decomposition Site in the H. J. Andrews Experimental Forest, a Visitation

Below thick moss and fungi and the green leaves
and white flowers of wood sorrel, where folds
of phloem hold termites and ants busily gnawing
through rings of ancient light and rain, this rot
is more alive, says the science, than the tree that
for four centuries it was. Beneath beetle galleries
vermiculately leading like lines on a map
to who knows where, all kinds of mites, bacteria,
Protozoa, and nematodes whip, wriggle, and crawl
even as my old pal's bark of a laugh comes back:
a recollection, perhaps, of Seattle when he appeared
out of a van with Tobias Wolff just as I was passing.
"Hey, everyone, it's Peter Sears!" I said to my friends
and ran up as he stood in his long, black coat,
not saying a word, his smile under the streetlights
deepening as Wolff and his moustache politely waited
while I gave Peter a pen to sign my arm, my friends
wondering what in the world a "Peter Sears" was.
He was the one always breaking others up
with deadpan cracks in that New York accent,
Yale poet who came west, Hugo student
and Stafford friend, writer in the schools, low res
prof, Oregon's laureate and Rivers's father.
"He's so morose you get depressed just hearing
his name," he said once about a poet we both liked.
Perhaps it's the rust-red hue of his cheeks
in the spill of woody bits. Or something in the long shags
of moss draping every down-curved limb. He'd love to be

right now a green-furred Sasquatch tiptoeing
among the boles of these firs alive since the first
Hamlet's first soliloquy. He'd love to shout
"Gotcha!" as he grabbed me from behind. He'd be
in touch, he said in an email, as soon as the doctors
cleared him. Then a sharp ache at the news on a website.
When this tree toppled, the science continues, its death
went through the soil's mycorrhizae linking the living
and the dead by threads as fine as the hairs appearing
those last years along Peter's ears, and those rootlets
kept rooting after. That email buried in my inbox.
Two lines and his name in lit pixels on my screen.
What if I click Reply? That's what he would do,
even out of place and time, here in the understory's
lowering light where gnats rescribble their whirl
after each breath I send. Hey, everyone . . .

A Moment Ago

you were following your steps
across the driveway, head bent
in the dusk toward one worry,
then another, and the day's last chore
in the plastic bag in your hand.

It wasn't a sound or a touch,
but something like the presence
of a memory that made you stop
and look up to find yourself
nearly surrounded by the dim
outlines of eight or ten deer.

And here you are, still, as if you've
stepped through the charcoaled
air into a scene on a cave wall
(the thin legs) where someone
long ago (the lifted, expectant head
and tense breath) tried to bring you to life.

Her Yarn

For all those blasting by at sixty-something
        on that two-lane to Scio, she'd have been
a chance look to the left as their chrome
        flashed—slight, gray-haired woman
sitting in the front window of a small house,
        head bowed to the pattern
she was winding her yarn through. On one side,
        a box her caregivers kept dropping
spools of all colors into, and on the other, another
        filling for twelve years with doilies. No longer able
to sow her garden with rows of corn and beans,
        all through her nineties, every day but Sabbath,
there she sat, sometimes getting a honk
        and wave. Any who stopped left with stacks
of doilies balanced in their arms to keep
        and to pass on to friends or neighbors.
No one asked her to make them,
        nor did anyone ever say, Love that much,
like light greened by leaves and streams
        interlaced, Love. Any in need, which was all,
always, she took into her wiry arms
        and squeezed. *I just love you so much!*
She had no curses to give for a life of working
        fuel pumps and fields, raising her two
red-haired boys, or even the time Charlie in a tractor
        loaded with carrots backed over her foot.
No one knows how many doilies she made.
        As long as breath moved blood and bone,
she wove the way she prayed. From Marion
        to Harrisburg, there must be thousands
stuffed into cupboards. From one person
        to the next, into hospice homes and through

churches, they made their way around the world,
        one even pinned to a wall in Turkey, says Loyd.
Of the many I have, I've never put one to use
        to hold a hot plate or vase, like this one,
this bicolored hexagon of triangles
        making green and violet stars in my hands.
Of all the strands my great aunt left, I'm one
        who can't build or wire the way my cousins can.
I remember, though, resting my hand
        on her head as she sits in rainy light, threading
my fingers through her hair like mist
        as wisps of her grace thread through this.

Opening the Curtains

After hours with pages in my hands,
glancing up at the gold splashes
of the leaves outside and to find that place
wisps of tea steam vanish into, I love
to hear the after-school, front-door slam
followed by thumps and unzips and swishes,
quick steps and the wall-muffled cupboard claps,
and I love that it won't be long

before their bright, untied, ready-
for-anything voices discover me listening
to their crowd-like stomps up the stairs where—
in the first moments after they'd gone—
I had thought to open the curtains for what now
was greeting them in its silent, slanting appearance.

Totality

Scent of pancakes lingering
in summery air, the family waits for light
to go away. The sisters
like buggy aliens in too-big glasses
want to know how much longer,
stuffed animals propped at attention on their laps.
Their father squats, snaps a photo,
a few more, then straightens and steps
around to a new angle. The oldest shoots
"You crazy stalker!" from her mouth.

Like light rays, they go as they arrive,
he knows, but can't stop himself
and aims for his father reclining in a lawn chair,
knuckly, carpenter's son hands
folded, eyes closed.

He remembers a pay phone's light
under a swath of stars when he swore
he'd never be back, never be here,
like this, again.

At last, the moon, that other,
farther hunter, begins to interpose,
and the rest of the family steps out to see
its dark disc nick more and more of the sun.

The last time this happened
he was his youngest's age. A dim memory
of warnings at school about going blind.
In their father's house, their father's church,
he and his sisters had already mastered
the language of omission.

Now where the sun was, the glare
of a single pupil rimmed in wild bright.

All the birds they hadn't been listening to
fall silent in the alien dusk. The creek
in earshot. A car. Why aren't they stopping?
At the sudden cold, he looks to his family
where they sit and stand about him, each lensed
by this brush of the great silence.
A prayer he thought he'd forgotten
moves once more in his mouth.

Only after he'd stopped going
to dialysis, as he was dying, did his grandfather
speak the words that had been blazing
for so long inside him.
He had looked directly into his eyes
and asked him and his sisters to be fully immersed
in the waters of Christ. He wanted to see all
his family again.

The moon begins to slide away, unslicing
what he has always simply called
the "sun." The birds and creek
go back to sounding like they should
and the family returns to conversation
and the house, the sisters their play,

leaving him alone with this man
whom he has always simply called "father"
still gazing into the plain brilliance of light
arriving as it will. Does he feel
its warmth? After so long obscured by silence,

is he, too, behind the blanks of those eyes,
looking for the words?

He remembers the old photos,
his father's unsmiling expression in shot
after shot framed by waves of thick, black hair,
stylish waves from the seventies

so white now they glow
like alabaster from another age,
another god. In the loose skin of the narrow hollow
between his neck and collarbone, a maze
like the wrinkled flow of time's branch-tapped waters.

He stays, content to watch his father
watch the sun. Through all
the open windows, not words but bright,
young laughter comes splashing forth.

Middle School

She throws open the door and hops out
with backpack and clarinet, then turns
to walk away as her glance
takes in her classmates

passing through the front doors,
bending to lock their bikes,
standing in small groups,
and in her face something happens,

she's someone else
who plucks off her pink headband
with its pink bow dotted with hearts,
checks to see if anyone saw,

and quickly hands it to me.
All last year and the years before,
since her first wisps of hair,
headbands have marked her

with colors, weeks going by
bright as wildflowers. Now a sideways look,
a brief lift of her hand, and bareheaded
she walks toward the school.

I watch every step I can, holding
the headband with the bow,
a pink U, a horseshoe. Not
for luck, I know, but letting go.

A Response to a Pair of Forest Plots

is my assignment. But all the firs
in the first that was clear-cut and
replanted huddle thick together
exactly alike, exactly where twenty
years ago each was boot-stamped
to grow into this big dark box.

And while the second was thinned
then—less crowded with intent, a little light
spilling through—I can't help
but see every sizable tree still grows
right where someone
shook a rattle can and sprayed.

Something else entirely
here in the roadside ditch

                                    in blue ruffled dabs
                    among the untidy
          grasses—wild
irises, where I kneel
                    to better see
                              white starbursts veined
with lines thin as moth legs
                              upon the splayed sepals—
and feel   the slight space
          held by the petals
                              that curl up and in like
tongues toward one other,
                    touch
          without touching,
                              and hold.

She Gathers Rocks

wherever she goes,
make that sticks—no,
leaves—which is to say

heads of flowers and hips.
More river than daughter,
her arms fill with treasures

of every trail. Hold this,
she says, to make us
her buckets, her pockets

already clack-and-bristle
full. It goes fast, they say,
and it was going as they

said it, for it's gone
into us counting to five
five times a day, saying,

"Time for bed!" "Time
to wake!" "Time to leave!"
And it's gone into her

quickening eyes and stride
that have left us
among all the things

she once believed
she couldn't leave behind.

The Seconds

Last patches of snow all but gone and first
wildflowers flecking the lawn, I walked out
to the shed and pulled open the door
with a woody squeak, and there, rising from the dirt floor,
surrounded by a dusty clutter of tools,

a little mountain, the kind of thing my daughters
might have scooped together in the fall and left
for the faeries if it weren't a perfectly conical accretion
of turds. What to make of such a thing,
holding the door, and beholding it in the spill

of the first light—and then I knew
the droppings. Here she was, my old dog,
that golden shuffle of paling wheat fields who'd retrieved
and licked clean how many rocks thrown from this hand?
What was left of her, here. What creature

had carried each dried nub from the yard's
far corners to form this strange cairn? There,
under the nail-hung weed whacker, my grease rag
on the floor pressed flat: a little bed I kneeled to touch.
Something had curled here in the gasolined nights

all winter as snow and more snow made a world
of white mounds. I walked around back,
searching for a gap, and stopped mid-step—
a big, squirrel-like bulk on my scrap wood,
the black, unblinking shine of a left eye

tilted toward mine. No glimmer of flight in that orb,
no twitch of scurry, only the deepest calm

as if the ages of the earth were taking my measure.
I felt like a pane of glass even as I took all I could
of it, its weight and whiskers and wide, rounded ears,

a long bottlebrush tail stretched out over my pile
of sawed lengths of lumber and plywood,
and later I would look for it in a book among my stacks.
That night, after I turned out the lights,
and my daughters asked for another story,

I told them of its midden while I sat on their floor,
becoming another dark shape among the heaps
of their clothes and stuffed animals; at first, "Eww!"
and then only the sounds of breathing as they remembered
their old dog, those restless slopes that passed

through their arms, the river sounds she made
licking those rocks to death. Let us not let go
ever, is what I took from your cave-wall stare,
wood rat, who would grab every bloody tooth
my girls have tucked under their pillows, pack rat,

who would make hill after hill of all the years
of their homework, vestigial historian, who'd cleave
to the locks of do-it-yourself haircuts and clutch
every tremor of their changing voices, their first words,
every shape and shade of their widening gazes,

and all the hard shit, too, the nights of no sleep,
the wet beds and fits and screams, slammed doors
and shaken fists (how long have you been with us?
how many iterations of you and them and me?),

even as you turned at last toward the woods

behind our house and slowly, one careful step
at a time, slipped away as if you'd already
snatched all the rain-colored seconds
from all the clocks that ever were or will be.

Her Present

beginning with a line from Dennis Held

Implacable, impeccably bereft of even the trace
of wrap and ribbon, Icicle Creek
glitters in the sun. In our swimsuits,
my daughter and I stand on a gray slope

of bankside granite as she counts—three,
two—until we leap as one, feeling our skin
warm through this June day's air
before the slap of snowmelt zero

sends us thrashing and gasping up
to hug ourselves half out of water,
the bare cold down to our core.
Fifty, I think, and might keep thinking

and shaking myself but for her glance
toward a cottonwood snag on the opposite bank
where, under a blue, cloud-hung sky,
an osprey perches by its talons clenched

on a dead branch, calmly watching us shiver.
When those first strange breaths filled her,
I saw the gangling animal she was, wonder
lighting her tilted face. Now, a drop

sparks from her earlobe as it falls to
the slow shatter of passing water·
and our shapes swirl into the other.

ACKNOWLEDGMENTS

Grateful acknowledgment to the editors of these publications in which the following poems were published, sometimes with different titles and in different forms:

About Place Journal: "Still Time"

AGNI: "Fish Like These"

Broadsided Press: "Timid as Any Herd Animal"

Dear America: Letters of Hope, Habitat, Defiance and Democracy (Trinity University Press): "What Will Keep Us"

Footbridge Above the Falls: Poems by Forty-Eight Northwest Poets (Rose Alley Press): "Traveling Again through the Dark"

The Georgia Review: "She Gathers Rocks," "We Could See"

The Gettysburg Review: "The Seconds"

Gray's Sporting Journal: "Emissaries"

Hampden-Sydney Poetry Review: "A True Account of Wood-Getting from up the Chumstick," "A Song for Today," "Daughter and Father in Winter," "The Math of Two," "Notes, Descending," "Opening the Curtains"

The Los Angeles Review: "hitch," "For Those Who Would See"

Poetry Daily: "She Gathers Rocks," "First Grade," "Contextual Education"

Poetry Northwest: "Stewards at Work"

Pontoon Poetry: "Bedtime Story"

Rattle: "Exactly What Needs Saying"

Shenandoah: "The Science of Spirit Lake," "Emergency," "The Skookum Indian," "The Empty Road Full of People," "Monsters"

Southern Humanities Review: "First Grade," "A Moment Ago"

The Southern Review: "Contextual Education," "It Wasn't the Laundry," "At the Log Decomposition Site in the H. J. Andrews Experimental Forest, a Visitation," "The Wren and the Jet at a Research Forest near Fort Knox,

Seventy-One Years since the Bombing of Hiroshima, Eight Months since the Photo of a Three-Year-Old Syrian Boy Facedown on a Turkish Beach, His Red Shirt, His Blue Shorts"

Sugar House Review: "Good Girl," "Her Calling," "John Carter of Mars versus the Void," "Her Present"

Tahoma Literary Review: "Middle School," "A Response to a Pair of Forest Plots"

Talking River: "Bedtime Story," "April," "Aubade," "Idaho, Maybe"

WA129 (Sage Hill Press): "The Scientists Gather at Mount St. Helens"

Many people and organizations have supported the writing of this book, and I thank them here, particularly the Spring Creek Foundation, the H. J. Andrews Experimental Forest, the Sustainable Arts Foundation, Artist Trust, Allied Arts Foundation, and Wenatchee Valley College, along with early manuscript readers Dennis Held, Rose McLarney, Jean-Paul Pecqueur, Betsy Aoki, Jack Johnson, Joe Powell, Simmons Buntin, Andrew Gottlieb, Elizabeth Dodd, Joe Wilkins, Allen Braden, and Kevin Miller, and readers of individual poems, Thomas Lux, Sandra Meek, Garrett Hongo, Jan Wallace, Joseph Green, and Kurt Caswell. Thank you to Julie Loehr and MSU Press and Mark Doty and Anita Skeen and her wonderful team at Wheelbarrow Books and the Residential College in the Arts and Humanities at Michigan State University. Thanks also to the editors of the 2016 Puschcart Prize Anthology for acknowledging "A True Account of Wood-Getting from up the Chumstick" with a special mention and to Vijay Seshadri for selecting "The Wren and the Jet . . ." as the finalist for the Lynda Hull Memorial Poetry Prize. "The Scientists Gather at Mount St. Helens" is for Fred Swanson and Charlie Crisafulli. "The Science of Spirit Lake" is for Tara Blackman and her team. "Emissaries" is for Andy Gottlieb, Chris Dombrowski, Whitney McDowell, Dwight Stoddard, and Steve Stefanides. "In Nez Perce Country with Kevin" is for Kevin Goodan. "It Wasn't the Laundry" is for Lucy Brewer. "John Carter of Mars versus the Void" is for Brian Rainville. "Contextual Education" is for Dan Stephens. "Her Yarn" is for Alice Henion.

SERIES ACKNOWLEDGMENTS

We at Wheelbarrow Books have many people to thank without whom Derek Sheffield's *Not For Luck* would never be in your hands. We begin by thanking all those writers who submitted manuscripts to the seventh Wheelbarrow Books Prize for Poetry. We want to single out the finalists: *A Case for Solace* by Liz Ahl, *Inventory of the Winter Palace* by Chris Forhan, *In Our Beautiful Bones* by Zilka Joseph, and *Some Girls* by Alison Luterman whose manuscripts moved and delighted us and which we passed on to the final judge, along with Derek Sheffield's manuscript, for his reading. That judge, Mark Doty, we thank for his thoughtful selection of the winner and his critical comments offered earlier in this book.

Our thanks to Lydia Barron, Alecia Beymer, Jillian Bowe, Jayla Harris-Hardy, Charlotte Krause, Kaylee McCarthy, Estee Schlenner, Fabrizzio Torero for their careful reading of manuscripts and insightful commentary on their selections, and especially to Laurie Hollinger, acting director at the RCAH Center for Poetry, who also read the manuscripts and provided the logistical aid and financial wizardry for this project. Sarah Teppen, a previous RCAH Center for Poetry intern, designed our Wheelbarrow Books logo which makes us smile every time we see it.

We go on to thank Stephen Esquith, dean of the Residential College in the Arts and Humanities, who has given his continued support to the RCAH Center for Poetry and Wheelbarrow Books since our inception. As we began thinking seriously about Wheelbarrow Books, conversation with June Youatt, then provost at Michigan State University, was encouraging, and MSU Press director Gabriel Dotto and assistant director/editor-in-chief Julie Loehr were eager to support the efforts of poets to reach a hungry audience. We cannot thank them enough for having faith in us, and a love of literature, to collaborate on this project.

Thanks to our current editorial board, Sarah Bagby, Gabrielle Calvocoressi, Mark Doty, George Ellenbogen, Carolyn Forché, Thomas Lynch, George Ella Lyon, and Naomi Shihab Nye for believing Wheelbarrow Books a worthy undertaking and lending their support and their time to our success.

Finally, to our patrons: without your belief in the Wheelbarrow Books Poetry Series and your generous financial backing we would still be sitting around the conference table adding up our loose change. You are making it possible for poets who have never had a book of poetry published, something that's becoming harder and harder these days with so many presses discontinuing their publishing of poetry, to find an outlet for their work. You are also supporting the efforts of established poets to continue to reach a large and grateful audience. We name you here with great admiration and appreciation:

Beth Alexander
Mary Hayden
Jean Kruger
Patricia and Robert Miller
Brian Teppen

WHEELBARROW BOOKS

Anita Skeen, *Series Editor*

Sarah Bagby	Carolyn Forché
Mark Doty	Thomas Lynch
George Ellenbogen	Naomi Shihab Nye

Wheelbarrow Books, established in 2016, is an imprint of the RCAH Center for Poetry at Michigan State University, published and distributed by MSU Press. The biannual Wheelbarrow Books Poetry Prize is awarded every year to one emerging poet who has not yet published a first book and to one established poet.

SERIES EDITOR: Anita Skeen, professor in the Residential College in the Arts and Humanities (RCAH) at Michigan State University, founder and past director of the RCAH Center for Poetry, director of the Creative Arts Festival at Ghost Ranch, and director of the Fall Writing Festival

The RCAH Center for Poetry opened in the fall of 2007 to encourage the reading, writing, and discussion of poetry and to create an awareness of the place and power of poetry in our everyday lives. We think about this in a number of ways, including through readings, performances, community outreach, and workshops. We believe that poetry is and should be fun, accessible, and meaningful. We are building a poetry community in the Greater Lansing area and beyond. Our undertaking of the Wheelbarrow Books Poetry Series is one of the gestures we make to aid in connecting good writers and eager readers beyond our regional boundaries. Information about the RCAH Center for Poetry at MSU can be found at http://poetry.rcah.msu.edu and also at https://centerforpoetry.wordpress.com and on Facebook and Twitter (@CenterForPoetry).

The mission of the Residential College in the Arts and Humanities at Michigan State University is to weave together the passion, imagination, humor, and candor of the arts and humanities to promote individual well-being and the common good. Students, faculty, and community partners in the arts and humanities have the power to focus critical attention on the public issues we face and the opportunities we have to resolve them. The arts and humanities not only give us the pleasure of living in the moment but also the wisdom to make sound judgments and good choices.

The mission, then, is to see things as they are, to hear things as others may, to tell these stories as they should be told, and to contribute to the making of a better world. The Residential College in the Arts and Humanities is built on four cornerstones: world history, art and culture, ethics, and engaged learning. Together they define an open-minded public space within which students, faculty, staff, and community partners can explore today's common problems and create shared moral visions of the future. Discover more about the Residential College in the Arts and Humanities at Michigan State at http://rcah.msu.edu.